RELIEVING CLASSROOM STRESS

A Teacher's Survival Guide

by

Franklin Schindelheim

First published by AuthorHouse 05/25/04

ISBN: 1-4184-5718-3 (e-book)
ISBN: 1-4184-2652-0 (Paperback)

Library of Congress Control Number: 2004092563

This book is printed on acid free paper.

Printed in the United States of America
Bloomington, IN

TABLE OF CONTENTS

To my wife Diane and my children, and all the children in whose life I made a difference, and who made a difference in my life.

INTRODUCTION

"Strategic Teaching and Response Techniques (S.T.A.R.T.) was developed as a response to a need for the classroom teacher to function at her maximum level. In the fall of 2001, I developed two courses for the New York City Board of Education and the United Federation of Teachers: "Effective Behavioral Management Strategies and Techniques" and "Relieving Classroom Stress". It wasn't too long before these in-service graduate courses became popular offerings for the New York City teacher. I made some interesting discoveries about teachers when I initiated these courses. Firstly, the starting date of these courses was only a few short weeks after the tragedy of 9/11 and the teachers who were instrumental in maintaining classroom decorum and curriculum development were traumatized by the catastrophe. Secondly, I noticed that teachers needed a forum to share their experiences and feelings about their profession. These classes and seminars soon developed into hands-on sessions where teachers were able to simulate typical and atypical classroom scenarios. Similar to a law school offering of moot court, the teachers were simulating real life classrooms. A teacher took charge of a classroom while other participants role-played children in her class. What began to develop was an adult's better understanding of what it was like to be a youngster in a classroom today. Teachers loved these role-playing exercises. Class participants were becoming quite adept at acting, and as an offshoot of these experiences, they realized that teaching in and of itself involves the art of acting and performing.

In my experience in offering these classes, I have also seen a pattern emerging when it comes to classroom control and management training.

It may best be described as benign neglect. In training the prospective teacher, much emphasis is placed on curriculum and philosophical ideas-yet the everyday approach to classroom control is left up to individuals. If you are in a homogeneously grouped school and you are fortunate enough to get that top class in the grade, then your management skills are focused on your curriculum preparation and keeping your students motivated. The occasional classroom problem is usually resolved immediately. Sometimes these solutions come out of moving a disruptive child or sending a letter home. Your colleagues that you encounter in the teacher's lounge, who are not as fortunate as you, talk about their classroom problems as if they are working in a different school or location.

One thing I notice when I teach my courses is that most teachers have difficulties in managing their classrooms sometime. Many of them are able to get through the school day hoping, sometimes vainly, that tomorrow will be a better day. When the "better day" never arrives, these professionals begin to re-evaluate their career paths. I have heard on several occasions that people are just fed up with the system they work in or that they have just "had it" with the teaching profession.

An activity that I encourage when teaching a class is called de-briefing. De-briefing is a counseling term. After counseling clients through a major ordeal or crisis, the counselor is encouraged to discuss the event with other counselors. This technique assists the counselor in bringing about closure; and allowing a vent for the feelings and tensions accrued during the prior counseling session. When I begin my behavioral management classes and seminars, I utilize this debriefing technique. I may begin by simply stating the rather benign comment: "Has anyone had a problem in class today?" Usually within a short period of time, the class begins to open up and a pattern emerges. Teachers from different areas and districts and schools will begin to vent and open up about the problems they encountered in their classrooms. They begin to realize that they are not alone. Their problems are shared with the rest of the class and solving these problems usually becomes a cooperative effort. It is hoped that this book will accomplish the simple goal of having teachers interact with their colleagues. Essentially, they will begin de-briefing and collectively share their successful behavioral management strategies with each other and ultimately achieve the goal of relieving classroom stress.

I recently had an opportunity to teach one of these courses to a group of teachers from several New York City school districts. The class consisted of twenty people; many were colleagues in the same school. In their collective efforts to devise the best classroom management strategies, they were able to not only share them with the class, but they developed turn-key approaches that they could convey to their colleagues in their respective schools.

I recognized a need for a systematic approach to behavioral management early in my career. I have had the unique advantage of informally observing hundreds of teachers. As a teacher, counselor, and video producer for educational videos, I witnessed these professionals in their own milieu-the classroom. I saw the product of their successes and indeed some of their failures. Exciting classrooms helped create excited and motivated children. Disorganized and poorly managed classrooms allowed for chaos.

As an impartial observer of these teachers, I wanted to know what substantive formula (if indeed one exists) makes a classroom buzz with excitement and positive learning. I knew what created the chaos. The lack of preparation, the perception of a daily grind and boredom and the lack of creativity were some factors that were evident in the failing teacher. It was those teachers who viewed their profession as a last resort. "I can't wait for the day to be over". "I wish I was in another profession". "I can't stand those kids"………These were the universal complaints of the ineffective and failing teacher. All too often the school administrator becomes involved with the ineffective teacher. This teacher's frantic calls to the office looking for the principal, assistant principal or dean of discipline present additional burdens to these administrators. Like the boy who cried wolf, they view these frequent summonses as just another problem that a problem teacher has developed.

The vital teacher is the individual that keeps her class motivated. These are the people that enjoy their profession, and their students' know that fact. They involve the kids in ways that are often fun, yet always respectful and courteous. They maintain students' trust and respect, and every day, their kids know a little more about themselves and the subject at hand then the day before. Their students are learning.

I also recognize the fact that classrooms are not utopias. Some children come to us with emotional baggage. We as educators cannot deny these children. Often they are in need of support that we alone cannot offer them. Many children have special needs and have been diagnosed as such. With the thrust of inclusion and collaborative education, it is incumbent upon the teacher to keep her class structured and exciting so the potentially disruptive child can be a vital part of the class and develop into a successful and contributing member of the classroom environment. One of the tools I offer the reader is how to maintain a good anecdotal record of the problem student. All too often teachers complain that the disruptive child in their room stays the entire year with nothing being done to remove that child. In my extensive years as an educator and counselor, I realized that the disruptive child's behavior difficulties were only addressed if the teacher used her/his observational abilities. These teachers maintained accurate and objective records of children's behavior. These records were necessary for administrators and child study teams to begin assessments of the particular child; and possibly place that child in the most appropriate educational setting. The same can be said for the child exhibiting learning disabilities. We would be offering a disservice to these children if we do not help in identifying their problems.

CHAPTER 1

WHAT'S DIFFERENT ABOUT MANAGING A CLASSROOM TODAY?

"Oh what a beautiful morning...." I couldn't help singing this famous line from that great Broadway show "Oklahoma" as I was driving over the Verrazano Bridge on this warm, clear late summer morning. I got to school a little early, about 7:45am. This particular Tuesday presented quite a few challenges to me. New York City schools were in session for about a week. The "honeymoon" was evident when I walked the halls of Seth Low Intermediate School. All the students were settled in and the teachers were involved in their lessons. As I stated, I had much work ahead of me on this particularly beautiful day.

The guidance office is a busy place at the start of school. The office is buzzing with students asking about schedules and classes and anything else twelve and thirteen year olds can think of to help assist them in life's simple chores. I had a second period appointment with a seventh grade boy I had met the previous year. Although he was a fairly well adjusted youngster, he needed school counseling to address his academic deficiencies. Indeed, Dominick was beginning to get a grasp on his organizational and study skills. We had a great counselor-student rapport and this session was devoted to the past summer's activities. At around 8:55am, my neighbor, another Counselor, Lorraine Carter, ran into my office and told me to turn on my radio. "It looks as though the pilot veered off course"...The commentator

1

was calm, yet we sensed urgency in his voice. For several minutes the news people were analyzing the events of this September morning. Moments later we knew what these events were. What is now known as the tragedy of 9/11 unfolded before our very eyes and ears. Those of us who live or work in New York City have been profoundly affected by those events. The Twin Towers proudly stood at the tip of lower Manhattan and were a welcome sign to visitor and commuter alike. They represented the best New York had to offer-majesty, grace; industry and especially a cool, yet aloof, dignity that said "We're NYC".

As those tragic events proceeded to unfold and began to sink into the collective psyche of everyone around me, I couldn't help but think back to a cold, snowy and bleak N.Y. City day in February 1993 when fifty-five Kindergarten children were stranded in the elevator and observation deck of those very same buildings in what was soon to be called the terrorist bombing of the World Trade Center. I was personally involved in helping to bring those kids home. As a crisis and guidance counselor in a busy, urban school district, I can safely say that I am pretty well trained to deal with every possible critical situation that befalls children, and after the events of 1993, I thought I would never witness a tragedy of that magnitude again. Obviously I was wrong.

Intermediate School 96, Seth Low (the school was named for an early mayor of Brooklyn) is a typical New York City Intermediate school. It is situated in the southern tip of the borough called Bensonhurst. The school has a history steeped in superior education. Notable personalities and dignitaries list Seth Low as their Alma Mater. Built in the early part of the 20th century, it was seen as an educational remedy to the burgeoning immigrant population that saw Bensonhurst, Brooklyn as a "good place to move to". Financier Michael Steinhardt, New York Met John Franco, and countless others have walked through the doors of this great school. I'm sure that we are still producing future senators, physicians, lawyers and baseball players. But as I walked the building on that memorable September day, I couldn't help but think how the events of this day would profoundly affect the lives of the kids in this school and countless other schools, not only in New York, but in the entire nation.

The events of 9/11 have made an indelible mark upon the adults and children of America, especially the children of New York City. When doing informal surveys of teachers in my classes, I find that many of them who were in the profession prior to September 11, 2001 have discovered that their students are indeed behaving differently today. They see a dramatic increase in classroom disruption along with an increase in erratic and sometimes bizarre behavior in some children. The reasons for this are many. I leave that to the researchers and scholars to delve into the root causes. Upon observation, however, I see that teachers today need more help in their classrooms. They not only need help in developing meaningful curriculum material, motivations and teaching skills; they need help in maintaining order in their classrooms.

CHAPTER 2

WHY WAS IT SIMPLER THEN?

In the 1950's when I was a youngster, I lived in the big city; indeed, most of my immediate world lived there too. Though the burgeoning growth of the suburbs had just begun with the returning GI of WWII and his young family, the suburbs were merely bedroom communities of the larger cities. Most Americans earned their livings in and near the metropolis. The economy was based on one-breadwinner families. Usually, dad would leave for work in the early morning and return home sometime in the early evening. With little exception, this held true. Of course there were economic disparities in American society. There were the rich and there were the poor.

No matter what socio-economic status one attained, one thing remained certain. Education-that is, attendance in school was mandatory. This simple law was as clear as crystal. It was set in stone. We had to go to school. In so doing, many of us gained some very important experiences from the people educating us. Most of our day was spent in a building that was somewhat antiseptic in appearance, and even more so in the aromas that emanated from it. I remember my first school as being a rather large and dingy building that reeked from ammonia and detergent. After much protestation on my part, my mother was able to finally leave me with the teacher and go about her daily activities of being a mother. Some of those activities included picking me up at noon, escorting me home and making sure that I had a nutritious lunch. By and large, city schools did not have big lunchrooms. Most children went home to eat.

That lunchtime became a ritual to children all over America. Along with our tuna fish or peanut butter sandwich, we were able to watch the afternoon offerings on our recently purchased black and white TV. In the nicer weather, our mothers or older siblings would walk us back before line-up so that we could play in the schoolyard. Life was simple to a child in the 50's. Surely, there were world crises and tragedies. After all, only a few years before, there was a war in Korea, and some years before that a major world war. But we Americans were happy and somewhat sanguine with our newly found prosperity. The three major networks on our TV's were paving new paths in the field of entertainment. Our parents constantly berated us for watching too much television, reading too many comic books, or simply not being conscientious enough about our studies and education. We were often reminded that they were working at twelve years of age and had to bone up on their studies all of the time. They told us that they wanted a better world for us than the world that they were born into.

I particularly remember my father being a voracious newspaper reader. New York had as many as eight daily newspapers. I think we had all of them every day in my home. One headline, in particular, always stuck in my mind: "Cold War Heating Up". What was a cold war? This was a term applied to the constant tensions between the super powers of the United States and the Soviet Union. Ever since the Korean War, which began in 1950, there was a persistent struggle between the two powers. The Soviet Union wanted to spread its communist system. The U.S. wanted to stop the spread of communism. Both countries possessed the Atomic bomb, and even worse, were developing bombs capable of decimating the world many times over; the dreaded Hydrogen bomb.

I think I first learned about these lethal bombs when my third grade teacher, Miss Fischer, explained the meaning of the air raid and shelter drill. What a fascinating topic for an eight-year old. She proceeded to tell her class that in the event of a nuclear bombing, we had to seek shelter. And where better a place for shelter than under our desks. Very simply, when we heard two gongs, we were to immediately stand and then dive for cover under our desks. We were told to stay in a crouched position on our knees with our arms protecting our heads. This all makes sense to me now. After all, during a nuclear holocaust, we must protect our heads from flying glass.

I particularly remember Mr. Wagner, the school principal, inspecting our class, making sure that we all attended to the drill instructions. When we heard another series of gongs, we were told that we could proceed with our daily lessons. These drills became part and parcel of every child's life in America. Though now we can scoff at the inanity and futility of an air raid drill in a nuclear firestorm, the powers that were in education felt satisfied that the students of America were prepared for a major crisis.

I remember the fall of 1962 quite vividly. I particularly remember sitting in my French class. Though it had nothing to do with the language of romance, my teacher, Mr. Koppelman, found it necessary to remind his students that a crisis of major proportions was unfolding before our young eyes. Though it would be the news event of the century, he exhorted that none of us would be around to read about it. He further added that our young firebrand of a president, John Fitzgerald Kennedy, would never back down to the Soviet menace and it's leader Nikita Khrushchev. It seemed that the Soviet Union was sending missiles to its client state, Cuba. This was right in our back yard, and Kennedy proffered an ultimatum: either the ships bearing the missiles retreat to Russia, or we will blockade their entrance into Cuba. This was the ultimate threat. We Americans trusted this young President, but we feared the worst. Mr. Koppelman seemed to enjoy his recitation of the week's events. The girls in the class burst into spontaneous hysterics each time the teacher told tales of nuclear destruction. We were on the precipice of war and devastation, yet here we were- in our high school French class, listening to this lesson on international polemics and debate, sensing that all too soon, our sheltered world of comic books, malt shops and Walter Cronkite would soon be obliterated.

Khrushchev, with all of his drama and histrionics, demurred; and in a short time the missiles began heading back to their country. I passed French, and Mr. Koppelman was able to tell his grandchildren about the Cuban missile crisis, and how it impacted on his students. Our young President, the President who promised so much to so many only lived one brief year after his confrontation with the Soviet Union. In the fall of 1963, John F. Kennedy was gunned down in Dallas Texas.

There are still many of us who remember exactly where we were when JFK was assassinated. I remember returning from school on the school bus, and some other students were yelling that the President was shot. They yelled at each other rather jokingly, and so I thought nothing of it. When I

7

disembarked from the bus, people were openly weeping in the street. The radio was on in my house, and my mother, too, was crying. Never in the history of the United States did a tragedy unfold before our eyes, as the assassination of President Kennedy. The electronic media was becoming more and more sophisticated. We were eyewitnesses to this collective drama that each of us shared. For the first time in history Americans were able to view, with shock and awe, their own destiny. Television presented accounts when none were previously available. On the Sunday following the assassination, Jack Ruby's shooting of Lee Harvey Oswald was viewed by millions.

The missile crisis and the assassination presented major implications to educators and the youth they were responsible to educate. These two crises, like no others in history, were brought into every classroom in this country. The question may be asked: Were our schools prepared to handle these critical situations?

In one situation, educators of the fifties and sixties would unequivocally concur that good shelter and air raid drill training were critical in the event of nuclear disaster. This is partly true. If the country were to be under attack, than certainly it was incumbent upon the school to train the student for the aftermath. Though we, as children, never understood the full implications of a nuclear attack, we may concur that the school did its job, though a yeoman job it may have been.

The schools certainly were not prepared to handle the crisis of the assassination of the president. Yet they did. They were able to do their jobs because of strong family support. Children were given a day off to mourn for their fallen leader. Many lessons were taught about the life of JFK. The entire country was in a state of shock. Families and friends became a safety net for the counseling needs of the millions of children who perceived the president's death as a death of a member of their family. The school's job in the 1960's was to educate. This job was done extremely well. Though we suffered two major crisis situations in a short span of time, the children of my generation had close-knit familial ties to get them through the tough times.

One thing remained constant for me; it was the feeling that I had about my teachers. I respected them and indeed I was in awe of many of them. The attitude of society was that students respected the educator! I know I wasn't the best kid. In fact I was pretty wild. During some of those notorious air raid drills, I was usually the child who slapped the backside of the kid in front of me. I was usually the one to get into trouble during recess. One particular event stands out in my mind----Linda Cole and Donna Andretti were playing jump rope. I ran into their twirling rope, swiped it, and proceeded to tie David Grayson up, using the technique of the mummy's undertaker ("The Curse of the Mummy" was a big hit in the movies). Miss Tucker immediately put an end to this nonsense. Her bark of "Franklin" echoed through the brick play yard like a roar of thunder. All the children froze in place as she proceeded to untie poor David. She approached me with all the grace and aplomb her two hundred and seventy-five pound carcass could muster. Though I trembled with fear, I refused to let her see me cry. ---- I was quite the impulsive kid, and truly couldn't help containing myself in certain situations. The mummification of David was just such a situation. As she lumbered toward me, I remember her words as if they were burned in my mind- "I want to see your mother tomorrow!!!!" When I gave my mother the letter, I knew what was to come. The punishment was swift and exacting. There was no explanation from me to justify my misbehavior (I thought it was just some frolic and frivolity). By the next afternoon, I was able to sit more comfortably when my mother, Miss Tucker, and I had a conversation about my malfeasance. My mother assured the teacher that this behavior would cease immediately. She also explained that my father had yet to be informed of my treachery. As I recall that conference wasn't very democratic. They did not allow me to offer any explanation at all.

There were other "bad" children in school. Larry Simons was constantly getting picked on and getting into fights. He was the school bully and fall guy all at the same time. When he acted out in class, the teachers wreaked vengeance upon him. If a lesson was being taught that Larry did not want to participate in, he was usually thrust into the farthest corner of the room-his back to the class. Mrs. Simons, Larry's mother, was looked upon as a poor, unfortunate soul who could not control this ten-year-old monster. Needless to say, today Larry has quite a lucrative practice in Sports medicine on 82nd street and Central Park West.

The point I am making is that we had a system of controls in place. As society became more complex, we gradually lost control of behavior management in our classrooms. The turbulent 60's gave way to the laid back 70's---the "Me" 80's---the X generation 90's. The classrooms in our schools reflect the mores, values and ethos of our society.

CHAPTER 3

TODAY'S FORMULA FOR FAILURE
(Or why it was simpler then)

Increasingly, the institution we call school has taken on a greater identity and persona. It is no longer just a place where children go to learn. Lunchrooms now are the places where the entire student body of a school eats. Because of the dual working parent home, children no longer go home for lunch. Many parents leave their homes early and therefore children are now eating breakfast in school. "Latch Key" and other after school programs are becoming more prevalent as society sees the need of the schools not only in educational terms but in custodial terms as well.

Although children do not realize it, they are being managed throughout the entire school day. Years ago school behavioral management was rather simple. On the grander scale of global catastrophes, children were to respond to adult authority as if the rules were "set in stone". The smaller everyday problems required simple discipline procedures enacted by stern disciplinarians in school and were almost surely followed up at home.

The 21st century presents a new era for American education. The teacher and administrator must be vitally aware of the prevailing attitude of society that the school is not doing enough to educate its' young. In this era of pervasive violence, cyberspace scanning and home grown terrorists, the educators of today must be able to address all the needs and demands of students growing up in these hectic times.

If MTV = 2:30 and SD=380, explain why MTV can never equal SD

The above formula is not a mathematical equation, but explains why Johnny can't read; pay attention in class; acts out and misbehaves…etc.

Can you figure out the simple paradigm of 21st century education?

Come on………It's not that difficult.

Hint. Think……….What does MTV stand for?

How about just plain TV?

Now you're getting warmer.

O.K. Give up?

Here's the answer.

MTV (Music Television Videos) videos are usually about two minutes and thirty seconds long.

SD (School day) is usually 380 minutes long.

Today we as educators are faced with a dilemma that is becoming more complex as technology continues taking over our lives. Kids are subjected to an unprecedented media barrage. Whether watching MTV videos, playing on Play Stations and X-Boxes or surfing the web, the attention span of the viewer is simply shrinking. Video producers and game makers are recognizing this fact and through enormous financial resources are creating more sophisticated presentations. Given all of this competition, how can we as teachers be expected to maintain classroom attention and excitement for an entire school day? Obviously we need to re-think our classroom management strategies. We are given the responsibility of educating our youth, yet we are not prepared with all of the necessary tools to succeed in that task. In my experience in training teachers, I began to realize that successful, vital, and effective teachers all use similar strategies. In their own unique ways, they are all performers. They are aware that their students view them as larger than life. They know that they cannot compete with attention grabbing distractions, but they know that they can certainly become an attention grabbing attraction.

CHAPTER 4

THE S.T.A.R.T. SYSTEM OF BEHAVIORAL MANAGEMENT
(*SUCCESSFUL TEACHING AND RESPONSE TECHNIQUES*)

Managing the behavior of a classroom of children is a skill that must be learned. If learned and practiced consistently, the teacher will have rewards beyond expectation. You, as an educator, will be in full control of your class at all times. Your energy will be spent toward teaching the content of your lesson. You will create a safe and healthy learning environment where children will thrive and flourish. Larry and Franklin are still around; the difference is that today they are bullying others with weapons. Creating an organized and well-managed classroom environment can give back the teacher to the children. Let's START now.

Critical situations arise every day in almost every public, and private school in America. The crisis may arise any time and be instigated by any number of extraneous factors. Any time a group of people is immersed in a contained area, any number of problem situations may develop. More often we perceive a crisis as one of major importance having an impact upon a large population, but critical conditions and situations occur every day in classrooms throughout the United States. Dealing with these critical situations in an organized and systematic approach will further add yet another tool to the educators' arsenal of proactive teaching techniques.

When they use a strong behavioral management technique, teachers are better able to derive the benefits of their profession- that is: teach so students will learn in a healthy environment. Handling behavioral management in an organized and efficient manner allows the teacher to be in command of her class at all times during the course of the school day.

Experienced teachers recognize the fact that students are subjected to various moods and outbursts. Classrooms today are microcosms of our complex society. Surely, one recognizes the fact that as society grows more complex; as media brings our problems to the forefront; as the close knit nuclear family becomes a vestige of our past, dealing with behavioral management in the classroom and the school is as relevant as the teaching of all curriculum areas.

Offering a simple approach to all teachers and administrators in dealing with any situation affords them an opportunity to further organize their school day and send their students home a bit safer and more mentally healthy then the previous day. Compartmentalizing a system into an organized approach that can be utilized in any situation (at any time during a school day, in any classroom, school and district) allows for true behavioral management.

The first word in the acronym S.T.A.R.T. is strategic. When you are in a classroom, everything that you do with children-your lessons, your discipline, your classroom management, and lastly, your very demeanor, must be thought out and strategically planned. Your students look you at as "larger than life". This may sound trite and somewhat corny, but just think about what happens when you run into students outside of the school. If they are with a parent, they usually act very shy and withdrawn and wish they would be anywhere else in the world, except where they are now. You, as the teacher, have the power to change the world-one child at a time. Use that power judiciously and you will make a difference. Learning to strategically teach and respond to your children will add greatly to your professionalism, and help you toward alleviating classroom stress.

S.T.A.R.T.
Successful Teaching and Response Techniques

There are four key components in this strategy:

- <u>ADDRESS</u> the situation.

- <u>INVESTIGATE</u> the situation.

- <u>RESPOND</u> to the situation.

- <u>COMMUNICATE</u>. Open all lines of communication.

CHAPTER 5

ADDRESS THE SITUATION

Ralph Kramden: "Just keep your head down
and address the ball".
Ed Norton: "Hello ball".
(HONEYMOONERS TV series, circa 1954)

A classroom is a busy place. At any one time, a teacher is able to keep the class occupied with various learning activities, all the while overseeing the entire class. Good teachers have the ability to keep their finger on the "pulse" of their classes. They know their students and recognize any problems that they encounter. They take into account several factors-they know the kind of home life a child has. They know when their students are sick, or merely feigning illness. If their students were absent, they usually know the reason(s) why. The teacher becomes familiar with students' school and homework habits, and recognizes the little nuances and idiosyncrasies that add to each child's individuality.

Let's look at a potential crisis situation and how a teacher could ADDRESS the situation.........

**Teacher addresses problem of
child who is emotionally
overwrought...........**

Edward Banner is a fifth grade teacher in Average elementary school in Middletown, USA. His teaching and behavioral management skills are exceptional. He truly represents what a teacher is in today's society. He has earned a Bachelors degree in education, and is working toward advanced degrees in educational administration and supervision. Mr. Banner is a tenured teacher and highly respected member of the Middletown community. His class is heterogeneously grouped with standardized test scores ranging from two years below grade level to the top national percentile. He motivates his students and brings his lessons to life with the zest and élan of a great teacher. Parents clamor to place their children in his class.

The child study team had tested Ernest, one of Banner's students, earlier in the year. Though the child was barely getting by in previous grades, Banner felt that the child was showing signs of perceptual and learning difficulties. Banner followed the prescribed course in assessing Edward's difficulties. He kept careful records of the child's performance. His anecdotal events of any unusual or disruptive behavior were carefully documented. He informed the parent through phone and in-person conferences on the progress of her child. In interviewing the parent, she stated that Ernest was always a very quiet child who always seemed to daydream. She remarked that Ernest had a definite dropping off of his schoolwork when his father left their home. She explained that her job was very demanding and that Ernest was often left home by himself to do chores and homework.

When the child study team did the intake of Ernest, Mr. Banner's input was invaluable to the evaluation. After several days of testing, it was found that Ernest did indeed have perceptual delays and learning disabilities. The team recommended that Ernest receive one period a day of intensive Special Skills instruction. Ernest seemed to be thriving in his new environment, and Mrs. Jackson, the Special Skills teacher, gave Mr. Banner all the necessary supportive materials that would help aid the youngster in Banner's room.

Early one morning while Edward Banner had the rapt attention of his class during a fascinating science lesson involving Sir Isaac Newton and the theory of gravity, he noticed a disruption coming from the area where Ernest was seated. In fact he noticed Ernest was not sitting at his desk, but under it. He went over to the child and asked what the problem was, Ernest proceeded to jump up, call Banner and the class names, run around the room, hit another child, tear up paper, and run out of the classroom. The class was astounded. At first they stared in disbelief. Some children began to nervously laugh while others started to raise quite a stir.

What the reader has just read is the development of a behavioral crisis in a classroom in Anywhere USA. Mr. Edward Banner could well be Ms. Banner or any teacher in Anywhere USA. Events such as the above occur on a daily basis, perhaps not as dramatic and animated, but, nonetheless, just as critical. The first and perhaps most important step in dealing with Ernest's outburst is <u>addressing</u> it.

Mr. Banner's first reaction in addressing the situation is to objectively <u>disassociate</u> from it. Sometimes a split second decision is needed to address a critical situation. Take the Banner predicament. He must address the situation. By stepping back, and objectively seeing the events unfold, the teacher can actually separate himself from the hysteria of the moment. Taking a few quick <u>deep breaths</u> is an excellent tool. Actually <u>physically stepping back</u> and <u>observing the entire event</u> is another good tool. Addressing the problem simply means that it is recognized and must be attended to.

When you address the problem properly, it will afford you the opportunity to <u>take charge</u> of the situation. It can be a matter of precious seconds or minutes, but once the progression of address and recognition occurs, the take-charge aspect of the problem will fall into place.

"Loco Parentis" [1]

For more than six hours a day, at least 180 days a year, a teacher is the responsible adult in a child's life until that child reaches the age of sixteen. The Latin term for this custodian-ship is "loco parentis" literally translated as "the stead (place) of the parent". Essentially this means that the teacher assumes the responsibility of the parent while the child is in the care of that teacher. When educational reform and mandatory public education began in the late 19th and early 20th century, it was understood that the teacher would assume the parent's responsibility in the education of the child. Though various state and federal laws have changed regarding age and grade requirements, it is still accepted by educators and the general public as well, that the teacher maintains this primary responsibility. Hence when addressing the situation, it is incumbent upon the teacher in question to address the safety issue first and foremost. The safety of students and staff has become the most important factor in school crisis management today.

> According to a recent survey by the *National Education Association:* During every school day at least 100,000 students tote guns to school...16,000 skip classes because they fear physical harm.... 40 are hurt or killed by firearms.... 6,250 teachers are threatened with bodily injury, and 260 teachers are physically assaulted. Are these grim statistics, or another startling reminder that society's ills are trickling down to our young?

Using our scenario of Edward Banner's class, the teacher must first address the safety issue of the crisis. He must ask himself the following questions in that specific instance:

1. Was Ernest agitated enough to cause physical harm to himself and others?
2. By running out of the room, did Ernest create a chaotic and potentially dangerous condition to the school at large?
3. Did the child's agitation cause the rest of the class to become frenzied and frenetic?

- *Split Second Decision*

---

1. The American Heritage Dictionary of the English Language: Fourth Edition. 2000

When Edward Banner saw the disruption in his class, his first response was naturally to investigate the problem. This is not necessarily the case. As stated before, the teacher must <u>address</u> the problem. Investigation will follow naturally. There are so many intervening variables in most chaotic situations that investigating first will further lead to more chaos.

When Ernest became disruptive, Banner had to thoroughly <u>disassociate his own emotions, fears, and instincts</u> and <u>look at the problem as objectively as possible.</u>

The teacher's <u>leadership</u> must permeate throughout the class at all times. The frantic children look upon him as their adult leader and derive confidence in knowing that fact. When Banner acknowledged the fact that there was a problem, he addressed it using the aforementioned techniques.

<u>Don't P.A.N.I.C.</u>

Do not <u>P</u>ut <u>A</u>ll <u>N</u>erves <u>I</u>n <u>C</u>haos. It's an interesting little mnemonic device, but quite true.

All too often people will panic and become frantic and sometime quite uncontrollable in chaotic and critical situations. Physiological as well as psychological reasons have been put forth for these fright and flight reactions. They are precursors to panic and further add to the chaos that ensues. When a crisis erupts, remember to disassociate yourself from the immediacy of the chaos. Take some deep cleansing breaths, physically step back from the situation and try to observe the event as objectively as you can. It is hoped that you will assume a leadership position with your students. Remember they are looking up to you for guidance.

> Several years ago I was a music teacher in a large New York City elementary school. My room was situated in a large and somewhat secluded corridor on the third floor of a five-story building. My only neighbors were a third grade class adjacent to the music room and a rarely used faculty lounge. One day, while returning to my room after lunch, I smelled smoke, and knew that it was emanating from the lounge. Though the door was closed, the odor of smoke was prevalent. I made the foolish mistake of opening the door. Naturally, opening the door was an invitation for the oxygen to satisfy the fire's need for nourishment. A blaze instantly flared up. At about the same time, the third grade teacher opened her classroom door and began to yell and scream.

21

I proceeded to remove the fire extinguisher from the wall and exhorted the teacher to remove her class as orderly as possible, and pull the fire alarm that was situated outside her room (there is a reason for those fire drills). She became more and more uncontrollable. At that point I shouted to her that the children's lives were at stake. Apparently that was the cue the teacher needed to snap her out of her hysterics. She immediately lined up her group and hurried them to the nearest exit, while pulling the fire alarm outside her room.

Whatever cue the teacher received at that point to snap her out of her own hysteria, I will never know. When I approached her afterward and asked her what was it that made her snap out of her panic, she replied that she could see a disaster unfolding before her very own eyes, and knew that she had to act to save her children. She related to me that my exhorting her to pull the alarm caused her to remove herself from the situation and essentially take charge. She then proceeded to take some cleansing breaths and ultimately remove her class form the dangerous situation

As the crisis unfolded, the teacher put all nerves in chaos--she panicked. By finally disassociating herself from the immediacy of the situation, she was better able to address the problem and ultimately lead her students to safety. She realized that at that moment the safety of her children was the most important element, and that she had to remove the children from imminent danger.

REVIEW-ADDRESS THE SITUATION

1. Deep breathing
2. Physically, step back
3. Observe entire event
4. Problem recognized
5. Take charge (freeze techniques)
6. Don't P.A.N.I.C. (put all nerves in chaos)

CHAPTER 6

INVESTIGATE

When a problem erupts in a classroom, there is always a reason for the problem. It is as simple as that. There must be a reason for an untoward situation to occur. Some problems and crises are predictable. Many are not. We are all familiar with the term "an accident waiting to happen". The same holds true for a classroom crisis. Naturally good behavior and classroom management skills on the part of the teacher could avert these crises waiting to happen. It requires simple logic to get to know your students and where best to situate them in your room. Sometimes the mere placement of a disruptive or inattentive child nearer to the teacher's desk can help that child better focus, thereby creating a healthier learning atmosphere for him. There are occasions, however, when the incident happened so quickly, and so violently, that a thorough investigation must take place.

We have discussed addressing of the initial crisis and how to deal with the situation. Remembering the key elements in addressing the situation: *Don't P.A.N.I.C. (put all nerves in chaos); disassociate yourself from the crisis at hand; take several deep cleansing breaths; take charge.* These steps allow you to better address the problem. Once the problem is addressed, you must find the reason for it.

**There is always a reason
for a disruption.............**

Albert Marano is a middle school math teacher. One day during passing, he noticed a commotion in Sheila Blank's art room. It seems that two boys were fighting. When Marano went in to break up the fight, one of the students told Marano to stay out of his "damn" business. Marano, a well-respected teacher at the school asked the angry boy to calm down and perhaps talk about the problem. The youngster responded with "I really don't care about talking. In fact I really don't care about anything". With that the boy angrily walked away and went to his next class. Marano followed and asked the English teacher, Mona Brown, if the youngster had that attitude from the beginning of the year. Ms Brown felt that Tony James had a learning problem, but seemed to appear extremely quiet and withdrawn all term. Marano asked for Tony's phone number.

That evening Marano placed a call to Tony's home. Tony's mother answered after the first ring. She seemed to be apprehensive and wary as to why Mr. Marano had called. Marano explained what had transpired with Tony that day and wanted to inform the mother that Tony appeared to have a problem. Mrs. James told Albert that since Tony's father had died three years ago he had withdrawn into a shell and would have occasional blow-ups and temper tantrums. She was having a terrible time coping and realized that Tony was having a tough time too. With that she began to cry. She told Marano that she would talk to Tony and thanked him for his concern.

The next morning Albert Marano met Al Sobel, the school counselor. He explained the Tony James incident to Al, at which point Al began seeing Tony on a regular basis. Tony's emotional progress was phenomenal. Al and Tony had hit it off instantly and within a few short weeks, Tony's marks and behavior improved dramatically.

Al Marano <u>investigated</u> the problem. He spoke to the child, interviewed the teacher, called the parent and referred the student to the guidance counselor. This act of investigation, which probably took about twenty minutes, saved a child's emotional life.

Simply stated, every school offers a safety net to the troubled child, whether it is through a child study team evaluation or referrals to the guidance personnel; but it is up to the teacher to **investigate** the problem and explore the avenues of resolution.

Reminder

Students who exhibit extraordinary and unexpected behaviors may be experiencing temporary or transient turmoil. Take into account that the behavior outburst is out of the ordinary and demands your immediate attention through <u>addressing and investigating</u> the problem.

REVIEW-INVESTIGATE

1. Disassociate yourself from the crisis at hand.
2. Take several deep-cleansing breaths.
3. Take charge.
4. Don't P.A.N.I.C. (Put all nerves in chaos)

CHAPTER 7

RESPOND

OK---You have practiced your techniques of addressing the problem. Investigating the problem with celerity and honesty qualifies you for your junior detective badge; the question now is how do we respond to the problem?

The key to good classroom and school behavior management is responding to the problems and managing the behavior of all the students. You want them to conform to your ultimate goal-that is teaching all of the students in the most satisfying and fulfilling means possible.

Much of this book so far has dealt with large-scale management and crisis situations. In dealing with the response aspect of START, we must also learn some important techniques that we can rely upon throughout the school day. Every one of these techniques may be adapted to any crisis or behavior management situation. Some are instant tricks that you will have a lot of fun using. Others must be practiced just as a good magician practices his sleight of hand. They can be practiced with your class or with a cafeteria or auditorium full of students. Always keep in mind that children have active and vivid imaginations. Explore these with your class as if you were teaching the most creative lesson of the day. Kids love to play. Just observe them during free play at lunchtime or during recess. The alert teacher recognizes that children group themselves and organize their own interesting games during these free play times. Your response activities may be viewed as nothing more than games where you give the directions and your class is part of your team.

Your response repertoire should have the provisos that you will always respond appropriately and professionally. Children will respond to you better when you keep those simple principles in mind. You will derive much satisfaction knowing that you will be in full control of every situation.

Respond with Praise

We all want to be praised. The little trick with praising children in our classrooms is to "catch them being good". I have heard, on occasion, teachers carping that they are not actors nor are they in the business of foisting praise upon undeserving students. This may very well be true. Teachers are not actors; but they should observe actors. When performing a role, the actor assumes a different persona. They are able to assume the character they are portraying. Teachers are on stage for an entire day. They must employ skills similar to those of the actor. As far as foisting undeserved praise, the incontrovertible fact is that every child can be "caught being good". When Johnny, the class clown, takes out his math book and begins his assignment, go to his desk and tell him: "Very good, Johnny, you are prepared. I am proud of you." Obviously, consistency is the key. Praise him often when you catch him being good. He will begin to live up to your expectations. What about the rest of the class? You are correct in assuming that it would not be fair to only praise Johnny. You have thirty other children that deserve praise also. Children know that this child may need this special praise. Certainly, praise all of them when they are worthy of praise; but understand that praising Johnny will help in getting him on your side.

Respond by being a Counselor

As previously stated, the teacher acts as the parent surrogate (loco parentis) for the entire school day. You are a role model for countless children, even if you do not realize that fact. Youngsters look up to you, not only for the instruction that you impart, but also for the ethics and ideals you present to them. Often a child's misbehavior, disrespect, or lack of discipline has root causes. We can safely assume that the troubled student that creates disruption in our room usually creates disruption in other areas of the school building. It is our job as professionals to help this child. Naturally, with proper documentation, a referral process can be initiated for a child in need of evaluation. This, however, is not the case for every student that is disruptive or disrespectful.

In my experience as a teacher and a counselor, I garnered a true understanding of just how important individualized counseling is in maintaining the student/teacher relationship. I recall teachers meeting me in a hall when I was with one of their particularly disruptive students. "Sure, he's good for you", they would inevitably state. It wasn't too long before I realized that those kids really were "good" for me. Often, when I observed these very youngsters in class, they were usually involved in their old tricks of disruptive behavior. What a great revelation. I know how to fix the behavior management problems in school! Of course, I'm being facetious. But what if teachers had an understanding with the attention seeker that made that child feel that he was getting all of the teacher's attention? Couldn't it be surmised, then, that this particular child will better respond to the teacher? The answer is obvious. Heap praise and affection on most anyone and they will better respond to you. Often when I counsel a student in an individualized setting I am vitally aware that many of them present poor self-esteem issues. One of my goals in these sessions is to build that person's self-esteem. A simple way of going about this is telling the person that they are important to themselves and others. Along with this, I often praise the student for assignments or chores that they have attempted. Use of praise and ego building are terrific counseling tools. In some instances, success is almost instantaneous. The same holds true in a student-teacher relationship. The students who act out in class, who create disruptions, who do not hand in assignments on time, are the youngsters who benefit from this one-on-one counseling strategy. Try to identify the problem student early, and ask him to see you at the end of a period for a few moments. Use a firm, yet understanding technique when talking to him. Tell him that you expect great things from him and that you know he won't disappoint you. Explain that you need him to be part of your successful class. Inevitably, these students will conform to your wishes. When he is part of the class and may begin a disruptive behavior, approach him and quietly reinforce what you spoke about in your private talk. Something like this may take place:

> Teacher (observes Alan disrupting his group--walks over to Alan): Alan, I know you can do this work. (Teacher immediately gives him thumbs up sign of praise).
> Alan: I wasn't doing anything.

29

>Teacher: Remember what we spoke about. I know you won't disappoint me. (Immediately gives another thumbs up and walks away)
>
>Alan: O.K.

The first response a disruptive student may offer is one of denial (e.g. "I wasn't doing anything"). Your job is to turn this type of response around and re-focus on your one-on-one session. Conclude with your expectations of positive behavior ("I know you won't disappoint me.") and don't allow for the student's response.

This is a terrific technique. Realize that it may take several attempts at these sessions, but if you are consistent in your approach, you will have the student on your side.

Another benefit of these counseling sessions is that you will begin to really understand your students. I went over this technique with a group of teachers during one of my behavioral management seminars. They began role-playing the parts of students and teachers. One particular scenario stands out in my mind. One of the teachers' constantly brought up a child in her fourth grade class. She related that this child was in dire need of attention; and this usually created disruption during her lessons. She role-played the part of the youngster while I played her part, that of the youngster's teacher. The role-play went something like this:

>Teacher (The author): O.K. Jamie. Obviously you want to talk to me about something that may be bothering you.
>
>Jamie: (Role-played by the child's teacher) Why are you always picking on me? I never do anything, yet you're always picking on me.
>
>Teacher (The author): I am not picking on you Jamie. Don't you know that when I am teaching the class, you're always involved in either talking to the other children, or getting out of your seat?
>
>Jamie: (shrugs) The other kids always bother me.
>
>Teacher (The author): Let's make a deal Jamie. When you feel the other kids are beginning to bother or annoy you, just raise two fingers. As soon as I see your fingers raised I will come over to you and see what the problem is. That way you won't have to worry about getting out of your seat.
>
>Jamie: O.K. I'll make that deal.

In the subsequent session, the teacher who role-played the part of the disruptive child shared some revelations about Jamie. She related that the one-on-one session went exactly as had been had portrayed in class. During their first session, they discussed the two-finger signal. It worked for a few periods, but toward the end of the day, Jamie had begun acting out again. She reinforced their conversation by quietly going over to Jamie and gesturing with her two-finger signal and reminding the child of what they spoke about. She gave the child thumbs up of acknowledgement. He responded by immediately folding his hands and resuming his work. The deal that they made had begun to slowly gel, and in a few short days, she no longer had to reinforce the newly acquired positive behavior. A simple look of acknowledgement was all that was needed for Jamie to positively respond.

The key to reinforcing any positive behavior is consistency. When teaching positive behavior skills to children, the teacher must constantly reinforce those behaviors. Also understand that there will be roadblocks and snags in getting children to positively respond to you, but your consistent reinforcement will pay off handsomely.

Responding to a major crisis

Sometimes, classroom stress can seemingly be overbearing. There are times that teachers would rather be in any other profession rather then their current career. Their very demeanor and responses in certain situations may have profound impact on their youngsters. All too often the teacher is concerned about maintaining classroom discipline and management, yet her response to certain crises may have major implications on the children she is responsible to teach. The teacher must be aware that there is a system of support in place in her school. Personnel who are trained in crisis management, student support, and staff development are available in most schools to help the teacher respond appropriately to any classroom crisis.

Barbara Barry is a third grade teacher in an elementary school in Newark, New Jersey. The school is large and there are four other classes on her grade. She is a good teacher who cares for all of her children. Often, her colleagues kid her about being a mother to thirty children plus two of her own. She loves her children and has a wonderful working relationship with the other teachers, especially the four on her grade.

One early Sunday evening, Barbara received a phone call from one of her class mothers. The news she heard was horrifying. One of her children, Steven James was killed earlier that evening. He was playing Frisbee with his mother near his home, the Frisbee was flung at him, and he missed, ran into the street to retrieve it, and was fatally struck by a passing car. The child was rushed to the hospital, but was pronounced DOA. The class mother who related the story could barely contain herself. Barbara dropped the phone and collapsed into a nearby chair. Steven was a pesky child who always seemed to want to go to the bathroom. The thought of her admonishing Steven for this trivial act further added to her grief. She started placing guilt upon herself. She thought if only she could have Steven at her desk tomorrow to explain how important he was to her. No sooner had she hung up the phone, when her principal, Ms. Joyner called her. She asked Barbara if she needed a substitute for Monday. Barbara emphatically insisted that she would be in school, but told Joyner that she would need arrangements made so that she could be at the wake and funeral.

After what seemed an eternity, Barbara met her class early Monday morning. Upon meeting her children she realized that she had to be especially strong. The news of Steven's accident had spread quickly and the children were visibly shaken. It appeared to Barbara that many had been crying for a long time. She wondered if her stoic manner with the children at this point belied her inner sadness. Ms. Joyner and Mr. Mannes, the guidance counselor, immediately met Barbara and the class at the classroom. Both commended Barbara for her strength during this time of grief. Mr. Mannes remarked that Ms. Joyner had addressed the crisis, and in so doing, maintained a sense of calm within the class. He proceeded to offer a grief crisis plan for Barbara and her class. He further explained that a team consisting of he and other counselors would be at the school for as long as the children needed them for bereavement counseling.

REVIEW-RESPOND

1. Professionally
2. Appropriately
3. With praise
4. Be the Counselor

CHAPTER 8

COMMUNICATE

The nature of the job demands that a good teacher be a good communicator. There are three kinds of communication that a teacher must employ during the course of a school day. They are verbal, non-verbal and written. After practicing some of the exercises in the S.T.A.R.T. program the teacher will be able to use any number of techniques involved in good communication with students.

Let's examine just how much communication between teacher and student goes on during the course of the average school day:

8:30----The class enters the room and the teacher has already placed the first period assignment on the chalkboard. (written communication).

During this time, a ritual of greeting and attendance is established. (verbal communication).

9:30-----Math lesson (verbal and written communication)

10:15---Class lines up for Gym (verbal)

11:30---Class returns to classroom to begin a new social studies project. Teacher must explain about cooperative learning groups. (verbal)

12:15----Class lines up for lunch. Procedures for lining up and lunch seating are reviewed with the class. Teacher uses various signals to remind students where to sit and remind about appropriate cafeteria behavior. (verbal and non-verbal communication)

1:15-----Silent reading for group I. Reading skills lesson for group II. Teacher groups children according to their functional reading proficiency. Teacher stresses directions and rules for silent reading. At the teacher's signal, the groups break up into their cooperative groups and silent reading places within the room (written, verbal, and non-verbal communication).

2:15-----Groups get back to their class position for a science lesson. The teacher signals for equipment assistants to distribute materials for the lesson. At the appropriate direction, the students will take out their science apparatus and place it on their tables. The teacher writes the aim on the board and proceeds to develop the lesson. (verbal, non-verbal and written communication)

3:00----Dismissal. Students know that at the signal they will line up and proceed to appropriate exits (non-verbal communication).

Communicate with By-Laws

The singularly most effective communication necessary in good classroom behavior management is establishing a <u>clear and concise set of by-laws</u>. This set of by-laws must be applicable the entire day and indeed the entire year. Think of your class as a mini-society. Societies enact laws for their citizenry. In the classroom society, laws must be enacted and followed so that order may be maintained. Similar to a democratic society, the classroom must be governed by an effective leader (the teacher) who establishes a firm set of rules for his/her class. You as the leader may establish your classroom laws with your students; it is still you who will maintain the laws.

Imagine a classroom that is lawless--it quickly becomes a chaotic and sometime dangerous place.

> I remember an incident that occurred many years ago. I was a young teacher and had walked into a sixth grade class to work on a music lesson that I had thoroughly prepared. The students were all over the room. Some of the kids were literally "climbing the walls". One particular child was on top of the wardrobe closet, tossing paper airplanes down to his fellow classmates. The teacher was calmly sitting at her desk, seemingly enjoying this chaos that was her room. I knew that, like me, she was a new teacher. I asked her if she needed any help in maintaining some order in the class. She shot back at me that the children were freely expressing themselves and according to the latest educational theory, she was the "free expression" facilitator. Obviously, no sense of order existed in that class, and as I recall, the kids behaved in that fashion for the entire school year. The teacher was not granted a position for the next school year. Fortunately for her, she was able to secure a good job for herself at the local community college. The last I heard, she was teaching education courses to aspiring teachers.

The above example represents a classroom that is out of control. It is obvious that the teacher did not maintain order. She allowed the situation to get out of hand until the class became totally uncontrollable. If the teacher would have established a firm set of rules from the onset of the school year, and if she had maintained a consistent approach to dealing with problems in her class, she would have derived the benefits of a successful teaching year. Ultimately the students would have derived the benefits of a sound education that year. Let us examine the laws, bylaws or rules that a teacher can effectively use in maintaining optimum communication with the class:

BY-LAWS OF MR JENKINS' FOURTH GRADE CLASS

1. ENTER ROOM QUIETLY AND WITH DIGNITY TO YOURSELF AND OTHERS.
2. RAISE HAND WHEN ASKING OR RESPONDING TO QUESTIONS.
3. NO GUM CHEWING IN SCHOOL.
4. ALL HOMEWORK MUST BE DONE ON TIME.
5. MEMORIZE THESE BY-LAWS.

Are these rules applicable for every teacher? The answer is obviously NO. Establish your rules so that they conform to your style of teaching. The important point here is that the rules must be fair and easily understood. It is senseless to have students memorize a series of inane laws and rules. Much of what can be said may be put into simple terms that the children understand. Make sure that your classroom rules conform to the philosophy and tone of your school and district.

Recently I had the opportunity to work in a very progressive school district in New York City. What struck me instantly was the informality between adults and students. The students called the teachers by their first names. They participated in open discussion without the use of the raised hand. The children displayed a healthy and happy attitude toward their school and teachers. Indeed, the school that I was in was one of the best performing schools in the city of New York. Yet, even at that school, which seemed so loose and informal, there were by-laws displayed in many classrooms. Some of them looked like this:

The By-laws of our class

1. DIGNITY
2. RESPECT
3. ASK QUESTIONS
4. SEEK ANSWERS

Though these tenets and principles may seem rather philosophical, the students bought into the program because the teachers constantly reinforced them. Make sure that when you establish the by-laws of the class, you are comfortable with them. You must also be able to refer to them and enforce them whenever necessary.

<u>EXERCISE</u>

RESPOND TO THE FOLLOWING QUESTIONS:

1. What behavioral goal do you have for your class for the remainder of the school year?

2. Do you anticipate any specific problems that may arise with your class?

3. Is there something that is specific only to your classroom or teaching situation? (i.e. You are a gym, music or art teacher.)

First year teachers are to omit the next response.

4. Is there anything that you would like to change from the previous year(s)?

After you complete the exercise try to establish one or two key words in each response. In question #1 you were asked if there was a behavioral goal that you wanted to establish with your class. Let us assume that you want to teach them respect for themselves and others and you do not want fighting and squabbling amongst each other. Try to phrase the by-laws as such:
* Maintain a sense of respect in room at all times.
* No fighting and arguing in school.

Question #2 asked if you anticipated any specific problems with your class. You may have a strongly competitive and gifted group. A subtle but effective by-law may be:
* Allow others to express their views, as you would want your views expressed.

Question #3 addresses the specificity of your situation. You may have an animal lab in your class. Effective by-laws may be:
* Do not disturb animals.
* Feed the animals only when instructed.

Question #4 asked if you would like to change anything from previous years. After some introspection you realize that the constant drone of talking and chattering has been a problem. Here's an effective by-law:
* Always listen to teacher's instructions.

(One instruction could be: No talking or interrupting teacher)

Now that you have established your classes' by-laws you can communicate them in many ways:

Written: Make sure that they are visible and always posted.

Verbal: Review by-laws with students and make sure that they are memorized.

Non-verbal: Be able to refer to by-laws by a use of hand signals. One finger may be law #1, two fingers, #2 etc.

In reviewing the schedule at the beginning of this chapter, the reader can now put the important part of the puzzle in place. The schedule seems so fluid and manageable. It truly will be if the teacher uses a strong, consistently reinforced set of by-laws throughout the day. Through the use of effective communication skills, whether they are verbal, non-verbal or written, the teacher will further derive the maximum benefits from his/her profession.

EXERCISE

Establish a set of by-laws for your classroom. Make sure they are appropriate for your class. Also make these by-laws work for the entire school year. Be consistent.

1.

2.

3.

4.

5.

Write by-laws on chalkboard.
Have students memorize class by-laws.

REVIEW-COMMUNICATION

1. Establish By-laws for all students that will be reinforced.
2. Verbal
3. Non-verbal
4. Written

CHAPTER 9

RECOGNIZING THE NEEDS OF THE DIFFICULT STUDENT

The following activities were specifically designed for the teacher to better gain understanding of the disruptive student. When we realize the forces that impact upon children, we are better able to handle the emotional outbursts and disruptions that affect the equilibrium of the class. After you do the next series of S.T.A.R.T. exercises, take some time to introspect about your answers. Discuss the answers with colleagues. Reflect upon them carefully. Try to acknowledge your mistakes in your dealings with the difficult student. Remember, there are often reasons why children act out or seek attention. Many of these reasons are obvious. The following exercises will help better prepare you in dealing with a difficult child.

"Walk in your students' shoes"

Think of a difficult student with whom you have dealt and write a brief answer to the following descriptions and questions as if YOU are the student.

1. Describe your home life. Include whom you live with.

2. What encouragement do you get from people at home for your efforts in school?

3. Describe your school experience. Include your strengths and weaknesses: academic, social, and behavioral.

4. How do you feel about teachers?

5. How do teachers feel about you?

I have assigned this exercise to my behavioral management classes since the course inception. Below are some of the more common answers to the questions and descriptions that have been elicited from teachers' perceptions of the difficult student. I have attempted to present the most common type of response. It is interesting to note how the responses illustrated are similar to yours.

Response to #1--- Describe your home life. Include whom you live with.

I live at home with my mom, grandmother and my older brother and younger sister. My mother works and my grandmother takes care of us when we come home from school. I have not seen my father since he left my mother five years ago.

Response to #2--- What encouragement do you get from people at home for your efforts in school?

I get no encouragement from my mother. She is too busy working. My grandmother is ill and always going to the doctor. My older brother is working and going for his GED. My little sister is good in school. My mother and grandmother give her encouragement all of the time.

Response to #3--- Describe your school experience. Include your strengths and weaknesses: Academic, social, and behavioral.

I am failing English and Social Studies. I am barely passing Math and Science. I am doing OK in Gym and Music. I have a few friends who are always getting in trouble with me. I am always getting poor behavior marks.

Response to #4--- How do you feel about teachers?

I like some teachers, but not too many. I like the dean of discipline (even though I am always getting into trouble).

Response to #5--- How do teachers feel about you?

Teachers don't like me. They're always blaming me for my behavior and threaten to call my mother. I like the dean of discipline, even though he is always calling my mother and grandmother.

Compare the typical teacher response to yours. You may begin to notice some similarities. In describing the home life of the difficult youngster, your student may indeed have family issues such as a broken home; drug and alcohol abuse; child abuse and neglect, etc. Thinking about your responses to the questions will better afford you the opportunity to understand that when this child arrives at school, there can be a potential overload of emotional "baggage" that is played out in the classroom. Poor behaviors, withdrawal, depression, anxiety, family illness, are just a few issues that this difficult child may bring to your classroom.

The student may be trapped in a downward spiral of academic failure. Often the self-esteem of these children is affected, and certainly that infringes on positive learning experiences. They feel that there is no way out, and that success in school is not important in their lives.

The disruptive student's perception of his teachers is almost universal. Most of these responses represent poor student/teacher relationships. The aforementioned student cited the dean of discipline as one of his favorite teachers—one that he likes. It is not an irony that the person responsible for meting out disciplinary punishment is the person that this student likes the most in school. Behavioral scientists claim that habitual misbehaviors persist because they are reinforced………."If repeated punishment were effective, children would stop their unacceptable practices. The fact that they do not is an indication that the "punishment" they receive is reinforcing".[2]

2. Edwards, Clifford H. -4th edition (2004). *Classroom Discipline and Management*: Wiley/Jossey-Bass

"More flies with honey than vinegar"

You have seen several students today. Think carefully about the response to the following questions.

1. Can you recall your reactions to students' questions today?

Yes____No____

2. Can you recall your reaction or response to students' negative behavior today?

Yes____No____

If you answered 'yes' to question number 1, list your response or reaction to students' questions.

If you answered 'yes' to question number 2, list your response or reaction to students' negative behavior.

3. Did a child speak nicely (courteously) to you today?

Yes____No____

4. Did you speak nicely (courteously) to a child today?

Yes____No____

If you answered 'yes' to question number 3, recall what the child might have said that you consider a courteous response.

If you answered 'yes' to question 4, recall what you might have said to a child that was a courteous response.

The "More flies with honey than vinegar" exercise asks you how you responded to your students and how they respond to you. In question # 1-- Can you recall your reactions to students' questions today? Many respondents were able to answer in the affirmative. Of course, they usually recalled their reactions to their questioning of their students. Many stated that they felt fulfilled when students answered their questions correctly. However, wrong answers usually were not received as well.

Almost all of the respondents in my classes answered "yes" to question #2-- Can you recall your reaction or response to students' negative behavior today? Usually their responses were peppered with phrases such as "I got angry", "I yelled at the student", "I punished the youngster", and "I felt helpless". Very few respondents answered that they ignored the behavior. Yet, according to B.F. Skinner, the father of Behavior Modification- When inappropriate behavior that was once reinforced is resolutely ignored, it is often extinguished, that is, weakened to the point of disappearing.[3] It would be wise to conclude that simply ignoring students' negative behavior on our part will create benefits in the long run.

Questions #3 and 4 refer to your methods of responding to your students' and, correspondingly, their responding to you. Many respondents to these questions noticed that when they were consciously aware of speaking courteously to students, the students, in turn, began to speak courteously to them. The simple adage-"One can get more flies with honey than vinegar" certainly rings true. By simply conditioning yourself to speak courteously to your students, they will respond to your commands in a like manner.

3. Edwards, Clifford H. -4th edition (2004). *Classroom Discipline and Management*: Wiley/Jossey-Bass

A profile of a difficult student
Answer questions 1 through 4 about this child.

Hi Ronald. You are an eleven-year-old (fifth grade) male currently attending P.S. 500. The school is located about three blocks from your apartment building where you live on the tenth floor with your Grandmother, Aunt and two younger siblings. Your mother died when you were five years old. You have lived with your Grandmother ever since. Your hobbies are drawing super heroes and singing. No one knows about your singing ability (you would be embarrassed if they heard you sing). You like to "fool around" with the kids in your class and often enjoy showing off in front of them. They think you are funny. For that reason you have developed a reputation in your school. They think you have a lot of problems. You generally do not like the adults in P.S. 500. They are always calling your Grandmother and trying to get you into trouble.

You have had these problems since the first grade. The school suggested to your Grandmother that you should be tested for special education placement, but she told the school that you were smart and refused to have you tested.

Last Thursday, during a boring assembly, you got into a fight with Billy (he's in the class next to yours). Billy called your mother a name and you just couldn't stand that. You were placed in in-house suspension for two days for fighting. When you came back you failed the spelling and math tests, but you just don't care. You hate school, the kids and especially the adults. They're always lecturing you and telling you that you had better shape up and they never saw a kid like you. You shrug your shoulders at them and you tell them that you just don't care.

1. Have you ever encountered a student like Ronald?

2. If you answered yes to the previous question, what sort of behavior did that child manifest?

3. Do you think it is unusual to have students like Ronald in your class?

4. What strategies do you use when you encounter a student like Ronald?

A profile of a difficult student is a good starting point for you to begin analyzing the needs of your difficult student. When you read the description of Ronald, you begin to understand the complexities of this child. The youngster describes the fact that he likes to sing and draw. If you have a child like him in your class, utilize these talents and help him flourish. Often, an adult's recognition of a youngster's talents may propel the child to new heights of self-esteem.

Ronald relates that he has had problems in school since first grade (note that Ronald was five when his mother died). His Grandmother has refused special education evaluation. All too often children are identified as needing evaluation for learning or behavioral difficulties, yet the caregiver may present resistance.

A common response from children who present difficulties as the above child is "I don't care". The fact of the matter is that the child <u>does</u> care. Often these children say they don't care because they find it easier and comforting to isolate themselves from adult authority by that response. When dealing with children such as Ronald, use S.T.A.R.T. strategies that will contribute to building his self-esteem. Also, be aware that helping a child like Ronald is a team effort. You will need to enlist the aid of the pupil personnel team (guidance counselor, social worker and psychologist).

You can't do it alone

All too often, children bring problems into the class that may be too overwhelming to address through conventional methods. The difficult child and the learning impaired child may present too many issues for you to deal with using conventional strategies and methodology. For this very reason the United States Congress enacted P.L. 94-142 in 1975-The Individuals with Disabilities Education Act (IDEA). [4] The law stated that children with disabilities have a right to appropriate education in a least restrictive environment. In the thirty years that the law has been enacted, much progress has been made in addressing and recognizing the educational needs of the disabled child. Inclusion, team and collaborative teaching have presented major breakthroughs in the success of special education in this country. Once considered a stigma, special education in the U.S. has made major strides in affording all children an appropriate and vital education.

It is vitally important for the teacher to realize that when she suspects a problem that may be present in her students, she has a means to help this child. An important component of IDEA is affording students the availability of non-discriminatory evaluations. Skilled professionals perform these evaluations. Psychologists, social workers, intervention specialists, and speech therapists may be part of a team that performs testing procedures on children recommended by other professionals (teachers) or the student's parent (or legal guardian).

Thus far, this chapter has been devoted to your perception of difficult students and an effective strategy in dealing with them. Other strategies and tips are presented in this book. But sometimes they just do not work. Indeed, there are children who may present difficulties in our classrooms that we may address, but no matter what techniques and strategies we employ for some, we sense that we cannot help them, and the dreaded classroom stress takes over. Some children may have neurological impairments that hinder their learning. Others may be so emotionally unstable or disturbed that our recommendation for evaluation would benefit them. You might ask the question-How can I recommend a child for an evaluation? You know your supervisors are aware of children presenting problems in your class.

---

4. U.S. Department of Education (2001). *Twenty-third annual report to congress on the implementation of the Individuals with Disabilities Act*

Many have probably spoken to you about these children. Often your parent communications go unheeded. Many parents are either too busy or are in denial about their children's problems. If you were armed with the tools necessary to, not only, identify these children, but place them in educational settings that would be most beneficial and appropriate for them, you would be on your way to educational "Nirvana". You scoff at the thought. These children-the ones causing and manifesting difficulties, are going to be lost in educational quicksand-only to be thrust into the next grade, or become someone else's problem. But there is a way to begin to salvage these young lives. As previously stated, there exists a support system in schools that are in place to help the teacher identify the child in need of services. They cannot do it alone. They need the teacher's unbiased, and objective observations of students' behavior. This is commonly referred to as anecdotal reporting.

An anecdotal report is an objective report of a child's behavior and performance. In order to refer a child for evaluation, and special education placement, the testing team must be able to have these reports at their fingertips to assess just how the child is responding in class. When a teacher suspects that a child may be manifesting learning or behavioral difficulties, she must be able to report specific incidents that back up her referral. These reports act as observations of the children's behavior. They are created by the professional who knows the child better than anyone else in the school-his teacher. They must be very specific and objective. When you are making an anecdotal report, you are the camera and recorder. You will write what you observe, and avoid any subjective comments or asides. If you are writing an anecdotal about Alex's running out of the room, do not add any comments about the child. If he ran out of the room, you will write-"Alex ran out of the room". Do not write – "Alex, acting rambunctious as usual, ran out of my room". Comments such as that are unprofessional and may place you in a compromising position with the administration. An anecdotal record is to contain observations as well as actions taken. You may want to report that you called the vice principal about Alex's bolting from the room. The following is a sample blank anecdotal record. You may use this as a template or design your own. Make sure that the child's name, date of birth, class, date and time of incident are on these forms. Also, be sure to have an action taken section on this report. Understand that you are in charge of your own destiny. Part of this empowerment is making sure that you have every tool available at your disposal. It is important to realize that not every behavioral management tool is aimed at specifically modifying behavior and getting children to conform to class or school wide behavior plans. The fact that you have the anecdotal recording procedure in your arsenal of tools will further help you to relieve everyday classroom stress.

Sample Student Anecdotal Report

Teacher Name: Helen Pelen

Student Name: Jimmy Smith

Class: 607

Student Date of Birth: 2/27/92

Date of incident: 2/6/03

Time of incident: 11:45 am

Describe (in detail) student behavior:

While the class was lining up for lunch, Jimmy rolled on the floor and refused to get up. When I approached him, he shouted to me that I was an idiot and should "mind my own business". I proceeded to summon Ms. Prince (assistant principal). When she arrived, Jimmy quickly got up and threatened her. He said: "I am going to kill you if you call my mother." Jimmy was then removed to the main office by the school security guard.

Action taken:

I called Mrs. Smith at noon. In our conversation, she related to me that Jimmy eats candy for breakfast, lunch and dinner. She said that she knows that too much sugar is bad, but if she doesn't give it to him, he locks her in her room and threatens to kill her. Ms. Prince related that she is recommending Jimmy for testing with the Child Study Team.

Blank student anecdotal report (use this template for your anecdotal report)

Teacher Name:

Student Name:

Class:

Student date of birth:

Date of incident:

Time of incident:

Describe (in detail) student behavior:

_____

_____

_____

_____

_____

_____

_____

_____

Action taken:

_____

_____

_____

_____

_____

_____

_____

_____

CHAPTER 10

TIPS AND STRATEGIES

The following tips and strategies were gathered over the course of my many years observing successful teachers. Use them sparingly. Use them in conjunction with your own <u>S</u>uccessful <u>T</u>eaching <u>A</u>nd <u>R</u>esponse Techniques. If any instant tip works especially well, make sure that you adapt it to your particular teaching situation and integrate it into your battery of successful teaching responses.

This is a good game you can play with an early childhood class.

Getting your class to "Freeze"
"The Museum of Natural Children"

This is an exercise that a teacher may practice with any size group.

Establish a word or cue that will get your class to immediately freeze and respond. Some teachers will actually use the word-"freeze", while others would wish to use another word, phrase or cue such as a desk bell or clicker. The object of this exercise is to have the class give you complete, undivided attention whenever you cue them. For younger children I used to play a game called "Museum of Natural Children". At the beginning of the year, I explained that we would play a game to see how well we can freeze.

The dialogue went something like this:

"Boys and girls we're going to play a game of pretend. We are going to be a class in the early part of the 21st century and a group of 24th century visitors from a far away planet have come to visit us. Let's make believe that they happened upon a school museum and let's see how well we can pretend that we are all part of the museum exhibit. When I say freeze, I want everyone to pretend that they are statues frozen in time." As you cue the children to freeze, be sure to keep reminding them "they are the best museum statues in the whole world".

You will marvel at the response you will get. Practice this "freeze" game with the students. It is an enjoyable and interesting way to get their attention.

Attentive Distraction

Here is a great tool that works wonders in getting your student's attention. I actually devised this many years ago when I was a band teacher and realized that the necessity of counting the cadence of a particular song to the band was important in developing the rhythmic scheme for that song. I subsequently began using the counting technique to classes when they were becoming chatty, unruly or distracted.

In today's busy classroom, it is not unusual to find the students seated in groups. Many guided reading lessons are culminated with the students working cooperatively in groups. While the teacher is working with one group, it is not uncommon for another group to begin to talk and sometime interrupt the other students. Here is a technique that really works. Try it. Announce to the students that when you count to three you want them to give you their attention; fold hands; continue working, etc. You begin "One, Two, Five, Seven..........Three". You get the idea. You are gaining their attention by saying the unexpected. You told them that you would count to three. Ultimately you will say the number three, but by saying numbers out of order they immediately give you their undivided attention. You are actually distracting them from other activities so that they can focus their attention on you.

The Point System

Establish <u>a point system</u> for work well done.

(e.g. Tell your students that you have established a weekly point system and that anyone who achieves twenty-five points a day is eligible to receive a Good Performance, Student of the Week, or Outstanding Attitude certificate at the end of the week).

Make sure that you keep a good record keeping system of all points credited to your students. The amount of points themselves may be arbitrary. What is important is that you remain consistent throughout the year in assigning the points.

Some terrific class rewards may be pizza and ice cream parties; a Friday afternoon video session; a class achievement certificate; a one night homework furlough; a grab bag.

6-401 POINTS
You will need a total of 14 points for
this week's reward.

Week of 6/1/2003

Monday	3
Tuesday	4
Wednesday	3
Thursday	2
Friday	3
	15

The illustration shows how your weekly point chart should look. Obviously, your class achieved the goal (14 points). Now you will need a reward for having achieved that goal. Perhaps the class is expecting a pizza party. Enjoy!

Parent Communication

*Letters home. One of the most effective ways of maintaining a well-behaved classroom is keeping in touch with home. If you make a concerted effort at the very beginning of the school year to contact the home of each student, it will make your job of maintaining a strong and well-behaved group a lot easier.

* An important note on home communication.

Parents are too used to hearing from the school when a child is misbehaving. If you establish the attitude that parents are an important part of the education partnership, they will appreciate hearing from you all of the time. It is vitally important for you to economize on your time when communicating with the home. If you are writing a letter than use the sample communication home letter as illustrated on the next page. If you are calling home keep your call short and simple. Explain to the parent that you call all of your students' parents and that you know how important they are in the education of their child. Tell them that if they have any questions they should feel free to call you at the school on your free period. Encourage the parent to attend the PTO meetings as well as all parent-teacher conferences. When your students know that their parent has been in touch with you from the very beginning of the year, they get the feeling that you mean "business". Stress to the students just how interested their parents are in hearing from you.

Sample parent letter introducing by-laws

Date:

Dear Parent,

I would like to take this opportunity to welcome your son/daughter into my class this year. I am positive that this will be a productive and rewarding year for both you and your child. Each year, I establish a set of by-laws for my class. I review these by-laws with the students and I expect that the students will follow these simple rules. It would be in everyone's best interest if you reviewed these by-laws with your child so that your child may advance in his/her pursuit of educational excellence. Here are the by-laws of our class:

1.   ENTER ROOM QUIETLY AND WITH DIGNITY TO YOURSELF AND OTHERS.

2.   RAISE HAND WHEN ASKING OR RESPONDING TO QUESTIONS.

3.   NO GUM CHEWING IN SCHOOL.

4.   ALL HOMEWORK MUST BE DONE ON TIME.

5.   MEMORIZE THESE BY-LAWS.

Thank you for your cooperation,

Mr./Ms._____

CHAPTER 11

S.T.A.R.T. FUN STRATEGIES

Make your classroom fun and exciting. Kids love to have fun. Childhood is about play. Toys and games are the major children's industry. When the teacher understands that she can be a constructive and major influence to the children's sense of play, it will be much easier to manage the class.

The following S.T.A.R.T. Strategies are sure-fire tried and true educational activities and games that you can play with the class to make for a well-managed day.

Demonstrate your class' ability with the "Performance".

In order for this exercise to work successfully, you must collaborate in advance with a colleague or supervisor. Explain to them that from time to time you will be calling them into your class to see them in action. This is not meant to be a write-up of a lesson or an observation. It is meant to be used as a behavior management tool.

Next, explain to your class that you are so proud of them for a particular accomplishment that you can't wait to show them off. Tell them that you would love to call in Mrs. Jonas, the assistant principal, to see the remarkable project (lesson, group discussion, play rehearsal, etc.) that you have been teaching them. It is extremely important that you build up the group's accomplishments. Be flowery in your praise (e.g." I know you can do it"; "Keep up the good work"; "Mrs. Jonas will flip out when she sees this"; "You truly are a great group"...etc.)

When Mrs. Jonas enters the room, you will address the class through Mrs. Jonas. Here is some sample dialogue:

"Good afternoon Mrs. Jonas and welcome to the best sixth grade class at the Monroe school. How do you like the way they look? Did you notice that Darlene has been doing some beautiful written work on the board?" (During your collaborative meeting with your guest, instruct her not to say anything at first, but to look around the room in awe-struck fashion.) You would be amazed at how many supervisors enjoy this exercise. They will milk it for all it's worth. Some may even be nominated for the Oscar.

The object of this exercise is to create a spirit of collaborative effort with the students. When you praise them through your guest, you will get the feeling that they and you are in on a private little joke that only you know.

Almost everyone wants to be praised. The class will derive a tremendous pleasure from this praise, not only from you, but also from the invited guest.

Do not use this too much, but you be the judge on how often you'll utilize this tool. You will find that it has tremendous impact on the class, and you will always be able to refer to Mrs. Jonas' visit when you are continuing with a particular lesson or activity.

Note that a student (Darlene) was specifically mentioned. Try to praise your difficult students immediately. They will be caught being good and attempt to model the better behavior.

Team "Jeopardy"

Like the TV show, this game involves facts. The respondents do not necessarily have to phrase responses as questions, but it may add a bit of the TV flavor to the game if the students' phrase their responses as questions. The rules for a class are rather loose. You may divide your class into two groups, or you may form the groups any way you desire. It is important that you must have two groups.

Next assign a captain from each group to come up to the board. The children will love to be the captain. Tell them that your rules insist that the captain be well behaved.

Draw a three-column chart on the board. Choose three popular topics and place them at the top of a column. Now vertically place the following point values to the three columns. In row one across, place the number 10. Row one questions are each worth 10 points. Explain that 10-point questions are very easy. In row two, insert 20. These 20-point questions are neither hard nor easy. Tell the students that they are so-so. The third row contains the hard questions. These are the 30 pointers.

The team that scores the most points on the board wins the contest. Note that there is a total of 180 points on the board. Obviously, the team that scores more than 90 points will win the round. Explain that the captain will pick the point value of the question and the category. Further explain that in order to qualify for the question, no one is allowed to call out. If a team member raises his/her hand than the captain may pick that member. If the respondent gets the question right, than you will erase the point value of the question, and insert the team name in that same box. If the respondent gets the question wrong, you simply erase the point value of that particular question, but losing points will not penalize the team.

Here is a sample playing board with subjects that I have chosen. You may use any subject that you wish. Try to integrate curriculum areas into your subject spaces.

Set up the playing board thusly:

SCIENCE	MATH	HISTORY
10	10	10
20	20	20
30	30	30

11-a

Try to prepare as many questions as possible well in advance. Remember a great way of reviewing the day's or unit's work is to frame all of your questions around areas that you have already covered.

Let's look at a sample game with questions based loosely on a fourth grade curriculum. Naturally you may adapt your questions to any level and subject area.

- Divide your class into two groups and designate names for them. Let's say you call them the Dodgers and the Rams.
- Choose two team captains who will pick the categories for their respective teams.
- Write the above table on the chalkboard. (See 11-a)
- Flip a coin or choose which team goes first.
- At this point have the captain choose a point value and category. Assume the captain is the captain of the Dodgers and he chooses math for 10 points, erase the 10 and if his team gets the question correct, insert the Dodgers name in the 10-point box under the math category. The sample question could be: What is 12x6? The designated team member responds with the answer-72. Now let us assume the opposing captain decides on a thirty-point science question. You ask a difficult one, but use content from something that you know you covered so far this year i.e. "What does a barometer measure?" If the captain chooses a student who has his hand up, but gives the wrong answer, be sure that you leave the 30-point box under science blank. At this point, the Dodgers captain chooses a category. Let's say she chooses history for 20. You might ask: "Who was defeated at Waterloo?" The captain proceeds to choose a teammate with her hand up, and she responds with the correct answer-"Napoleon". You must proceed to erase the 20 under the history box and fill in the word Dodgers. Thus far in the game the Dodgers are leading with a score of 30 to 0. See *(11-b)*

SCIENCE	MATH	HISTORY
10	Dodgers	10
20	20	Dodgers
	30	30

11-b

The Rams get a turn again. The captain chooses History for 30. If the Rams get this one, the game will be tied-if not the score will still be 30 to 0. The question: "Where did the Civil War surrender take place"? The captain picks Naquan. His response is "Appomattox Court House". He is correct and now the board looks like this:

SCIENCE	MATH	HISTORY
10	Dodgers	10
20	20	Dodgers
	30	Rams

11-c

The game continues until all the subjects are either filled in or blank. Add up the points for each team and designate the winner.

- Remember to give increasingly harder questions as the point values increase. Also keep in mind that this is an excellent learning as well as behavioral management tool.
- Encourage "perfect" behavior on this activity. You will be amazed at the amount of fun you and the students will derive from this game.
- Keep cumulative scores of the two teams throughout the school year. Establish an ongoing "jeopardy" class contest.

Team Tic-Tac-Toe

Here is another example of an educational game that may be played across the curriculum. Similar to "Jeopardy", this game keeps the students' attention at maximum levels as well as fosters gamesmanship and strong team competitive spirit. Set up your playing field on the chalkboard thusly:

1	2	3
4	5	6
7	8	9

(11-d)

Once again, choose two captains and set up the teams using team names. Let us simulate a typical tic-tac-toe contest:

You are a teacher of a sixth grade class of thirty-two children. You want to review a new social studies unit with them and you know that they love to play games. Divide the class into two teams and designate two captains. When you choose the captains, ask them to give you a name of a favorite team. Similar to "Jeopardy", they pick two team names—The Dodgers and The Rams. Draw a team chart on the chalkboard as shown. *(11-e)*

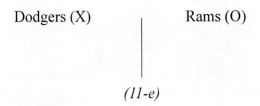

Dodgers (X)   Rams (O)

(11-e)

Now explain to the captains that The Dodger team will use the X, while the Rams will use O. Further explain that the object of the game is to get three consecutive symbols (X or O) in a row, horizontally, vertically or diagonally. Tell them that the rules of the game do not allow calling out and the only way that they as captains may recognize a player's response is if the player raises his/her hand. If that player gets the answer correct he gets his team's letter (X or O) placed on a designated spot on the tic-tac-toe board. The captain is the only team member who may pick the numbered spot on the board, but any team member may be chosen to respond as long as that member raises his/her hand. Tell the captains (so the class will hear) that if a member on any team calls out, than the opposing team gets a free turn. At this point you will understand how healthy competition amongst your students is a strong behavioral management tool for your class. When you allow the captains the freedom and responsibility of navigating through this age-old game, you will begin to see wonderful things happening in your classroom.

Now choose your captains. Robert will represent the Dodgers and Allison represents the Rams. The game begins. Robert starts by choosing the "5" position on the board. You ask the question:

"Name a signatory of the U.S. constitution."

The Dodgers rapidly raise their hands (you covered the unit on the constitution last week). Robert chooses Jennifer. She responds with "John Hancock". She gets it right. You erase the "5" and now place an X where the 5 was placed on the board. *(11-f)*

1	2	3
4	X	6
7	8	9

(11-f)

It is now the Rams turn. Allison chooses the "1" corner spot. You ask a science question:

"Spell the word-biome." (This week's science vocabulary word)

Allison chooses Carlton who immediately raised his hand. He proceeds to spell---b-I-o-m. Oh Oh! Carlton left out the 'e'. Instead of Allison's Rams getting the O in the number 1 space, the Dodgers get another X. *(11-g)*

73

X	2	3
4	X	6
7	8	9

(11-g)

What a contest! You feel the tension and excitement rising as the children eagerly await the next question. They know that The Dodgers are one question away from winning. The game proceeds. It is Robert's turn. He chooses the 9 corner spot to win the game. The question: "What is the square root of 81?" Without hesitation Ernie of the Dodger team calls out the answer." Nine"-he shouts, unable to contain his pent up excitement. Robert quickly tells him he had to raise his hand. A collective sigh of disappointment gasps from the Dodgers as the impending victory was just wrested from them by Ernie's over-enthusiasm. The board now looks like this:

X	2	3
4	X	6
7	8	O

(11-h)

The game continues. Allison chooses the '7' corner. You ask:" Spell loquacious". Allison picks Fatima. She proceeds: "Loquacious… l.o.q.u.a.c.i.o.u.s, she haltingly says each letter. She got it right; and now Allison's "O" team is one answer away *(11-i)*.

X	2	3
4	X	6
O	8	O

(11-i)

The Dodgers must choose the '8' spot to block the Rams. Ernie chooses '8'. The question: "Name the third planet from the sun":

Ernie chooses Dawn. Dawn says "Mars". "No! The correct answer is Earth." The Rams win the game. *(11-j)*

X	2	3
4	X	6
~~O~~	~~O~~	~~O~~

(11-j)

The team chart now looks like this: *(11-k)*

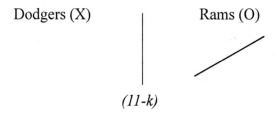

Dodgers (X)   Rams (O)

(11-k)

"Team Tic-Tac-Toe" and Team "Jeopardy" are terrific rewards and offer teachers excellent ways to motivate their classes. They should be employed sparingly, but when played, students should view them as rewards well earned.

Pick a Number

There is no greater power an adult can have over a child as that of being a psychic. Having the capability to read students' minds is a fascinating experience. Indeed, if it were really possible, a teacher would have her own TV or radio show. Obviously, I am not suggesting that teachers must have psychic abilities to succeed in their profession. But wouldn't it be a great way to get their students' attention in their class by reading their minds? I have previously discussed the necessity of utilizing performing and acting skills to pique the attention of your class. What I present here is another form of attention grabbing entertainment. Suppose you asked a student to pick a number from one to three, but he must only whisper that number to his neighbor. He proceeds to whisper the number to his neighbor. The class is awestruck. They can't believe you have these mystical powers. As he whispers the number, you proceed to the chalkboard; write the number two and quickly cover the number so the class doesn't see it. Ask the neighbor what number he was told. He yells out the number two to the class. You uncover your hand on the chalkboard and voila! You wrote the number two. The class is now stunned with amazement. You read their classmate's mind.

Here is how this mind reading trick works. I don't recall how I learned this trick; but an educational psychologist must have developed it. Apparently when you ask a youngster to pick a number from one to three, the child will invariably pick the number two. I have noticed that this is not always the case when adults are asked to pick a number from one to three. Statistically there is a one in three chance that the response will be two. However, since you are actually saying all of the numbers (1 to 3), there is a greater chance that the middle number of the series will be chosen. Once again, there is probably a reason for this statistical anomaly, but I have no idea what it is. I do know that kids love this little trick and you can use it for all it is worth. Make sure that you build up the trick as dynamically as possible. Here is a possible dialog:

Teacher:

O.K., how many of you know that I can read minds? (Usually the class will snicker and scoff at your query.)

All right then... I will need complete silence for this to work. As a matter of fact I need the best-behaved person to show me perfect behavior. O.K., Jeremy. I think we're on the same wavelength. Have you ever heard of ESP? That's extra sensory perception. That's mind reading. Pick a number from one to three, but do not tell anyone. Again---- pick a number from one to three. (Jeremy looks baffled, but you can tell he's thinking of a number.) Now, do you have a number? (He nods yes). Good! Now whisper the number to Barbara. (He follows the order and whispers something into Barbara's ear.)

(The teacher is still concealing the number that is written on the board.) O.K., Barbara. Tell the class the number that Jeremy whispered to you.

Barbara: He whispered the number two.

Teacher: (Uncovers the hidden number revealing the number two.) We're on the same wavelength Jeremy. I read your mind.

At this point, the students usually want the teacher to read their minds. Obviously, you only need to do this trick once.

You might inquire as to what would happen if Jeremy picked another number. Though improbable, it may happen. If it does occur, simply tell Jeremy that he's not on your wavelength and choose another student. The odds are certain that the number two will be chosen by one of the next two students.

Hand and Finger Signals

This strategy works great with kindergarten through fifth grade level children. It is less effective with middle and high school students.

Explain to your children that you are going to give them certain directions with your hands. You might say: "When I hold up two fingers, I want complete attention". After you give the direction, it is imperative that you practice the direction. Remember to use praise. Hold up two fingers. As soon as the children respond by giving you complete attention, make sure that you praise them. Use this strategy throughout the day until the children respond automatically to your two-finger signal. Use this strategy whenever you need your class' attention.

Make sure that your children are praised with the universal thumbs up sign. When you gesture to a child with the thumbs up, make sure you tell him how proud you are of his behavior. This silent form of praise instills a sense of pride in the child. Notice the look of affirmation on the youngster's face when you proffer this sign.

"One...two...three...Look at me!"

Here is a terrific early childhood strategy. It requires some rhyming skills, but with a little practice, you'll get the hang of it. I spoke about the Attentive Distraction technique previously. This strategy is quite similar. You get the children's attention by getting them to respond to your verbal rhyming commands. Essentially, you are getting their total attention and distracting them from other influences. The object of this strategy is to get the children to follow your directions through immediate responses to your commands. A typical scenario might proceed as follows:

Teacher:

Boys and girls... One two three, look at me. Now hands folded... Good! Hold it! Now the best will be put to the test... O.K... Now hands on shoulders...hands in air again, let's fold...now that's gold.

See if you can make up your own rhyming schemes to grab your class' attention. The children will love this little technique and you will derive much pleasure and satisfaction as they respond to your rhymes.

The Power of Suggestion

When I conduct classes and seminars in behavioral management, I find the biggest stumbling block to a well-managed class is that the students do not always respond to the teacher's commands. How often have I heard a teacher complaining that her lesson may be going perfectly until a child raises his hand for an insignificant reason (or for that matter a significant one)? This is a common complaint. Although a minor disruption, interference during an important part of a lesson is an annoyance we can live without. Those familiar with hypnosis and trance states are quite attuned to the importance of the power of suggestion. Simply stated, when a suggestion is presented, it is hoped that the subject will heed the suggestion. Similar to other strategies in this book (e.g. hand signal); the use of positive suggestions presented to a child or class will reap great benefits for the teacher. Let's look at a scenario where a teacher may employ the power of suggestion.

Scenario

Teacher is about to embark on a read aloud lesson with her third grade class. As she prepares her class for the lesson, she notices some children are restless and distracted. She gets their attention utilizing a rhyming or hand signal strategy. Before she begins her read aloud, she suggests to the class that they will pay attention to her and will focus on the book she is about to show them. She now suggests to the class that they will pay complete attention to the book she will be reading and that they will completely focus on the book. She repeats the suggestion of focusing on the book. She repeats the suggestion at least three times. Here is a typical dialogue for this scenario:

Teacher:

Boys and girls, today I will be reading a book entitled "The Ugly Duckling" by Hans Christian Andersen. Before I begin, I want everyone to pay attention to the book I will be reading to you. Once again, I would like everyone to pay attention to the book I will be reading to you. Very good! Pay careful attention to the book I will be reading to you.

The use of repetition reinforces the suggestion. In this case, the teacher is asking her class to pay attention. The desired goal should be met by using this strategy. When imparting suggestions, never ask the children questions like, "Do you remember what I asked you to do"? Obviously, the children would respond with correct answers, but by asking questions you are undoing the original suggestion. That would be—"Pay attention to the book I will be reading to you". You will find this strategy to be a very practical way of getting your point across.

You will find this strategy to be particularly helpful when you encounter a child who may not be listening to your instructions. Get the child's attention by using any of the strategies mentioned in this book. Attentive distraction would be a good one. Tell her to pay attention when you count to three. Naturally you will say numbers out of sequence until you say the number three. At this point, explain to the child that she is to pay attention and listen to you--repeat the suggestion several times. In a calm, yet authoritative voice, repeat the suggestion for the child to listen to you. At this point you have reinforced the necessary suggestion for the child to get back on track. You have imparted positive suggestions to reduce the child's distractibility.

CHAPTER 12

CALMING DOWN A KID IN CRISIS

Ideveloped this particular strategy early in my career. As a woodwind and brass musician and teacher, I had to develop breathing techniques. One of the key elements in playing a wind instrument or singing is called diaphragm breathing. This means that the woodwind, brass and voice student must be able to maximize the volume of air he inhales so that he can produce enough wind for his particular instrument. Diaphragm or belly breathing is a technique where the musician inhales as much air as possible while expanding his abdomen (hence the diaphragm causes the lungs to maximize the volume of air). Beginner students who practice this method of breathing often experience a light-headedness, at which point they are advised to stop the breathing exercise, and resume it at a later time. There is a similarity between this breathing technique and meditative disciplines such as Yoga and Tai Chi. These techniques assist a person to get in touch with his inner-self through meditation. The breathing exercises help to achieve that goal.

When I encounter an emotionally overwrought child, I try to leave him enough space and proffer a suggestion that will aid in distracting him from his present state of crisis. I would say something like this:

> "Look at my hand, Alex. Look at my hand... Take a deep breath and look at my hand. Good. Breathe deeply again and let it out slowly.... Good. Very slowly...take another breath.

> Let it out slowly… Very slowly…look at my hand and take
> another deep breath…. Let it out very slowly…"

This strategy works extremely well when breaking up a classroom fight. Usually when two children are engaged in fighting, a crowd of onlookers surrounds them and general chaos ensues. If the fight should break out in your classroom, use strategies we have covered in this book:

- Address the problem (e.g. you are at your desk preparing to escort your class to the auditorium. As they are lining up, you hear an inordinate amount of noise as the children run toward the rear of the line where you notice two children, Raymond and Luis flailing at each other).

  Do not P.A.N.I.C. (put all nerves in chaos)

- Respond by stepping back for a split second, taking a deep breath and moving toward the melee.

- Investigate the problem. Once again, this requires a split second decision (You determine that Raymond seems to be the antagonist).

- Communicate by calling the child's name. As soon as you do this, immediately say: "Look at my hand". Repeat this suggestion several times and hold your hand up and away from the fighting children. Do not attempt to physically break up fighting and flailing children. All too often, teachers have sustained substantial injuries when breaking up fights. Usually when you offer a suggestion in a firm voice, the child will respond. At this point, add that you want the child to take a deep breath. Repeat this suggestion several times until you notice him responding to your suggestion. Eventually, he will respond to this suggestion. Allow the less aggressive child to go back to his seat, or place in line. Explain to the children that you will get to the bottom of this problem shortly. At this point you escort Raymond to a space where he will continue to "cool off". Now it is your turn to contain yourself. Take some deep cleansing breaths, let them out slowly and proceed to do what you do best---that is teach.

This is a terrific strategy for calming down a child with a tantrum or in crisis. Try not to restrain the child. Make sure your commands are calming. Hold a hand up so the child will be able to see it and reinforce focusing the child's eyes on your hand while you tell him to take deep breaths. The child will usually calm down within a short period of time. Once the child is calm, continue to offer suggestions in a very soothing and soft tone. Tell him that he will begin to feel better shortly and at that time you will discuss what upset him.

CHAPTER 13

IT WORKS FOR ME!

The effective teacher utilizes a potpourri of tools at his/her disposal. In this book, I have demonstrated some proven and very effective tools to assist the teacher in relieving classroom stress. Their effectiveness has been proven many times over a career that has spanned decades. Find a style and develop that style so that you have a firm grasp on your professional responsibilities. If a particular technique is not working after many consistent attempts, then it may not be the correct technique to utilize with your particular group of children. You will ultimately find a technique that will work for you. Your job is to make sure that you consistently use techniques and strategies that will aid in your goal of becoming the most effective teacher that you can be.

We are in a profession that tests our skills all of the time. Often, at the end of a particularly trying day, we may actually question our very reason for continuing to work with youngsters. You might have had a day where nothing seemed to go right. You were prepared for all of your lessons and classes, yet the day turned into a nightmare. You felt as if you had failed yourself and indeed your students. Do not despair. This is a normal reaction. You are not the first teacher to experience this fleeting sense of failure, nor will you be the last. The key element to lasting success in the classroom is good classroom and behavioral management skills. These skills are acquired through practice. Use the strategies presented in this book and explore what will work for you. Make sure your classroom presents a safe and nurturing environment. Make it a place where children want to be. If you use classroom by-laws, make sure that they are in effect all of the time. If you present competitive events with your class, make sure that the competition is healthy and fair. If you play games with your students, make sure that they are fun. The techniques and strategies derived from this book will contribute to your success as a teacher, and hopefully, make your job more enjoyable.

A while back I had the opportunity to meet a teacher by the name of Joe Durso. Joe is one of the most interesting people I have met in my career in education. He had just begun a new career as a math teacher in a rather large urban middle school in New York City. Joe was an Assistant District Attorney in New York City and was longing for a career change. In addition to his career as an attorney, he was also a world-class athlete. He was the 1984-92 United States handball champion, having been cited in the "Sports Illustrated" Millennium issue as one of the top 100 New York City athletes in the 20th century.

I was the chairperson of the pupil personnel department and Joe and I developed a friendship. Joe would often come to my office to discuss matters of the day. He told me of his travail with some of his math classes. He felt he couldn't teach the youngsters because they "were out of control". Indeed he was right. Joe could not get a handle on classroom management. We would often discuss particular children in his classes that were creating disruptions. There were more names on his list than I could care to remember. It was getting so bad that Joe was coming to me every day for moral support and help. He felt his career change was becoming a disaster and began to rethink his professional plans. I knew I had to help Joe formulate a classroom management plan. But before we could enact any sort of successful plan, I made it clear to him that he had to maintain a persona that exemplified success and control. He had to change this prevailing attitude he had of defeat and failure if he were to succeed as a teacher.

We had conversations about his training as an attorney. I remember asking Joe how he had performed in court. He reflected that court was different. He was prepared and knew that a courtroom was a place that allowed for drama and histrionics. I knew Joe was a world-class athlete, and asked him how he felt about competition. He stated that he loved the game and looked at it as his own stage where he could perform his athletic feats. He showed me some videos of news programs that he appeared in. Joe was quite the athlete, but also quite the performer. Joe and I began to explore the similarities of his past career and endeavors and his current classroom situation. It did not take long for him to realize that he was a performer on stage all of the time with his students; only now his students were viewing him as a mediocre actor who really did not get a handle on his profession, and certainly wasn't able to interest them in his attempts to teach. We reviewed successful techniques. We set up classroom by-laws. We reviewed lesson preparation. I went over S.T.A.R.T. exercises with him. He practiced them with his classes and soon there was a transformation. As Joe met his successive classes, he began to notice subtle changes. His disruptive students were "quieting down". He was beginning to present successful math lessons. His parent/teacher conferences and phone calls were now beginning to stress the positives of his students. His lessons were becoming exciting. The students enjoyed the daily praises of their teacher. Joe was holding Team Jeopardy and Tic-Tac-Toe competitions. I often observed the students vying for the precious team captain positions for their respective teams. I saw kids performing sophisticated mathematics equations as if they were attaining their next achievement level on their video game consoles. I observed class point charts in Joe's room. Some of them had esoteric team names, while others had class numbers on them. Each chart had points posted. The students coveted these important point accomplishments and strove to achieve more points. When administrators or fellow teachers walked into the room, they were invariably greeted with a welcome that went something like this: "Good morning Mr. Schindelheim. Welcome to the best math class in this room right now. As a matter of fact they are in the process of receiving points for a job well done." It did not take long for Joe to feel revitalized. The students in his classes began to enjoy his approach and were having fun. Joe recognized that children learn best when a teacher can teach at his best level of performance. He became an effective behavioral manager and an excellent teacher.

Joe Durso is not the only teacher who has derived skills from the S.T.A.R.T. method of behavioral management. There are countless professionals who use these techniques and strategies on a regular basis. I am in constant contact with teachers whom I have trained in this method. They all concur. Their newly acquired behavioral management skills have given them a second wind in their profession. They enjoy teaching and are reaping rewards from their profession. Their students are learning and they know it. They recognize success on the faces of their students. Their colleagues feel the electricity generated in their classrooms.

When I see Joe in the halls now, I inadvertently remark to him that I hear great things about his classes. I told him that his classes performed extremely well on assessment tests, and kids were always happy when they exited his classroom. Joe would always respond with the simple phrase-"It works for me!" That phrase sums up this book. Make your strategies work for you. Don't give up on your goals. You entered a profession that is fraught with challenges and obstacles. Stay consistent; maintain self-esteem; and respect your students. It will work for you!

ABOUT THE AUTHOR

F rank Schindelheim has been an educator with the New York City school system for over thirty-five years. His vast experience as a teacher, counselor, educational video producer and teacher trainer has made him a vital resource in the field of staff development. He has written articles and appeared on national television as an expert on the subject of children in crisis. His lectures and seminars on classroom behavioral management are entertaining as well as informative. His graduate course- "Effective Behavioral Management Techniques and Strategies" is one of the most popular courses offered by The After School Professional Development Division of The New York City Department of Education. He is a professor of education at Touro College in New York City.

Printed in the United States
41808LVS00006B/586-597